Counting Descent
Clint Smith

൚

Write Bloody Publishing
America's Independent Press

Los Angeles, CA
WRITEBLOODY.COM

Smith, Clint.
1ˢᵗ edition.

Interior Layout by Kayla Shelley
Cover Design by Zoe Norvell
Proofread by Derrick Brown and Madison Mae Parker
Edited by Anis Mojgani
Assistant Editors: Madison Mae Parker

Type set in Bergamo from www.theleagueofmoveabletype.com

ISBN 978-1938912-65-8

Write Bloody Publishing
Los Angeles, CA

Support Independent Presses
writebloody.com

To contact the author, send an email to writebloody@gmail.com

MADE IN THE USA

Counting Descent

Something You Should Know 9

what the ocean said to the black boy............................... 10

For the Boys at the Bottom of the Sea 11

The Boy and His Ball 12

Soles 13

Ode to the Loop-de-Loop 14

My Jump Shot.. 15

Full-Court Press 17

what the cicada said to the black boy 18

Ode to 9th & O NW 19

what the fire hydrant said to the black boy 20

Counting Descent... 21

Keeping Score.. 23

a lineage.. 24

Counterfactual..25

Playground Elegy 26

Ode to the Only Black Kid in the Class 27

what the window said to the black boy 28

Saturday Morning Routine...29

When Maze & Frankie Beverly Come on in My House 30

Ode to the Drizzy Drake Hands 32

How to Fight 33

Zero Gravity.. 34

Ode to the End-of-Year 6th Grade Picnic 35

Passed Down 36

Dissection.. 37

For Charles 38

For the Boys Who Never Learned How to Swim............ 40

Beyond This Place.. 41

For the Taxi Cabs that Pass Me in Harvard Square 42

James Baldwin Speaks to the Protest Novel.................. 43

Canon 44

On Observing My Home After the Storm...................... 45

what is left 46

Lifeline 47

The Protest Novel Responds to James Baldwin........................ 48

The Men in Orange 49

How Malcolm Learned to Read... 50

From the Cell Block... 51

How to Make an Empty Cardboard Box Disappear in 10 Steps 52

Meteor Shower 53

Chaos Theory 54

No More Elegies Today.. 56

An Evening at the Louvre 57

An Inquiry... 59

Each Morning Is a Ritual Made Just for Us 60

Line/Breaks.. 61

When They Tell You the Brontosaurus Never Existed 62

Today I Bought a Book for You 63

Shout Out.. 64

It Is Early December in Cambridge 65

When Mom Braids My Sister's Hair...................................... 66

For the Hardest Days 67

Queries of Unrest.. 68

what the cathedral said to the black boy 69

There is a Lake Here 70

Notes 71

Acknowledgements 72

"I recognize no dichotomy between art and protest."
— **Ralph Ellison**

Gavin, none of this is possible without you. You showed me the way.

Something You Should Know

is that as a kid, I once worked at a pet store.
I cleaned the cages
of small animals like turtles, hamsters,
rabbits, and hermit crabs.
I watched the hermit crab continue
to grow, molt, shed its skin and scurry across
the bottom of the aquarium to find a new shell.
Which left me afraid for the small creature,
to run around all exposed that way, to have
to live its entire life requiring something else
to feel safe. Perhaps that is when I became afraid
of needing anything beyond myself. Perhaps
that is why, even now, I can want so desperately
to show you all of my skin, but am more afraid
of meeting you, exposed, in open water.

what the ocean said to the black boy

you know how to swim boy?
i know you can float
felt you bobbing along my surface
before you even knew you could

they say you just a conflagration
of bad intentions boy
they use me to put you out
don't want you burning this place down

again

they see
a little too much l'ouverture in you
a little too much turner
a little too much of what they already had enough of

what you see when you look at me?
you know how many of y'all I swallowed?
you just a drop of ink
on this canvass

boy

they call me blue because
they don't understand how the sky work
they call you black because
they don't understand how god work

For the Boys at the Bottom of the Sea

We are charred vessels
vestiges of wood & wonder
anchors tethered to our bows.
It is the irony of a ship burning
at sea, surrounded by
the very thing that could

save us.

The Boy and His Ball

The boy is bending down to hold the laces
tight between his index finger and his thumb.
Practices somersaulting the strings between
one another, his conductor's baton tossing
revolutions through the air.

Over   *under*
       through   *pull.*
Over   *under*
       through   *pull.*

Now, he lets the shoestring halos fall
on either side.
The cleats, when he runs,
dig themselves into the endless earth.

The soil spits upwards, black
streaks airborne
cascading into the jubilant wake
of the child.

His feet flourish around the ball, learning
the orbit of taut leather, the texture of low-
cut grass. The boy and his brown body
glimmer under a sun that showers

light onto every outstretched
blade. How when the boy dribbles, he looks
like he's dancing, how he's got
capoeira in his hips, how his feet
have never learned of fatigue.

Soles

You've been sitting at that desk a lot lately. Just you, those papers and pen. Feels like you barely use us anymore. We remember when your whole world relied on everything we did. We're the ones who made it so the other kids didn't pay attention to how many books you read but instead how fast we moved. We won the race to the fence and back every Tuesday in P.E. Left Eric and Calvin in the dust. Gave you something to claim as champion at a lunch table where pride was all you had. Sure, we'll admit it, we didn't always know how to act when the DJ turned up the volume. The beat got faster, and we made you look more hopscotch than hip-hop, more Urkel than Usher. But that was never in the job description. Still remember when you threw away the New Balance and first wrapped us in Air Forces. Walked into school with alacrity, the pure white sheen of Foot Locker glimmering like quartz—an indomitable sort of swag. Thought this would finally be the moment Alexis Sanders told you she really liked you too. But nah, you're still the big-headed kid who likes Star Wars and French architecture. We were always just an afterthought. Wasn't until you fractured your ankle that you realized what we meant. That we kept you standing upright when all this world has done is try to knock you over. When all you ever wanted to do is run.

Ode to the Loop-de-Loop

We've always had a strange
relationship, you and I.
You're a peculiar sort of sight,

how you look like the distorted
spine of an Apatosaurus.
A brilliant contortion

of steel and physics.
I'm not gonna lie, though.
You scare the shit out of me.

How you manufacture inertia
and sell it to the highest bidder.
How you simultaneously exist

as a masquerade of false gravity
and a centrifuge of boundless euphoria.
This was all more manageable

when you came in the form of
my Hot Wheels play set.
Somewhere I could preside

over your twists and turns,
govern the kinetic energy
between my hands.

But I see how you create a certain sort
of ecstasy. It's why people run to see
the photograph of their faces after

getting off the ride, to be reminded
that this sort of exhilaration is possible.
Tell me, at what velocity does joy travel?

Does it need a harness?
Or merely the right degree of force
to disentangle the fear from the rapture?

My Jump Shot

My jump shot be
>   all elbow and no wrist.

My jump shot be
>   asking what a follow through is.

My jump shot be
>   hard to look at.

My jump shot be
>   Medusa.

My jump shot be
>   the leftovers you don't really want to eat.

My jump shot be
>   the fridge that don't work.

My jump shot be
>   the sour milk in your cereal.

My jump shot be
>   getting picked last by the other jump shots.

My jump shot be
>   old spaghetti.

My jump shot be
>   gluten-free.

My jump shot be
>   Michael Jordan when he was seven.

My jump shot be
>   spending too much time in the library.

My jump shot be
>   making everybody else feel better about their jump shot.

My jump shot be
>   asking why we didn't stick to soccer.

My jump shot be
>   code-switching.

My jump shot be

       making people nervous just because it's a jump shot.

My jump shot be

       the only jump shot in class.

My jump shot be

       getting asked to speak on behalf of all the other jump shots.

My jump shot be

       wondering why people think all jump shots are the same.

My jump shot be

       explaining how jump shots come in all shapes and sizes.

My jump shot be

       sounding like it's talking about snowflakes.

My jump shot be

       a snowflake.

My jump shot be

       a home.

My jump shot be

       the only jump shot I've ever had.

Full-Court Press

I.

Mirabeau Ave. is alive with the bass of Cash Money Records & the pop
of crawfish boiling, their small bodies exploding inside skintight shells.

The driveway to our garage, & the rim that hangs above it, a slice
of suburb in this mixed income corner of the city. It makes our home

a centerpiece. Older boys come knock on the door,
balls tucked on hips, to see if I want to play. I am too

young, of course, to understand the false pretense of preteen youth—
to know they would have played without me if they could. All I saw

were the boys I admired standing on my porch, asking me to join them.

II.

The summer concrete sweats under our feet. My outstretched arms
crisscrossing the court, beckoning for a chance to become hero.

When the game is over & we sit along the sidewalk, they knock
the back of my shoulder, palms open, nod their heads upwards & say,

Good game, lil' nigga. When the boys leave, I saunter into the house.
Mom standing over red beans simmering on the stove, baby brother

crawling under the dining room table. I walk straight to him, chest still
full of interminable pride, pick him up & say, *What's up, lil' nigga?*

Mom's spoon of beans splatter onto the counter, the viscous sauce
oozing onto the ground. *What the hell did you just say?* I am

unprepared for this shame. I put my brother down, heaves
now breaking from his tiny chest. She comes over, grabs a handful

of my collar. *Boy, don't let me hear you say that again.* The beans boiling
over on the stove. A mess left across the floor.

what the cicada said to the black boy

i've seen what they make of you
how they render you a multiplicity
of mistakes

they have undone me as well
pulled back my shell & feasted
on my flesh

claimed it was for their survival
& they wonder why I only show my face
every seventeen years

but you

you're lucky if they let you live that long
i could teach you some things you know
have been playing this game since before

you knew what breath was
this here is prehistoric
why you think we fly?

why you think we roll in packs?
you think these swarms are for the fun of it?
i would tell you that you don't roll deep enough

but every time you swarm they shoot
get you some wings son
get you some wings

Ode to 9th & O NW

You hundred-year-old bastion of merriment
You crumbling icon
You hollow walls & sacrosanct floors
You kitchen where rice burned & whiskey spilled
You wondrous accident
You ephemeral cacophony
You first taste of adulthood
You crumbled piece of adulthood
You omnipresent laughter
You roommate shuffleboard
You millennial experiment
You eye of the gentrified storm
You Duke Ellington in a world full of yoga studios

Three years in your grasp & we watched
them turn the Boys & Girls Club
into happy hour
It's something about how you sit
on the corner
at the intersection
of where I learned to tell someone
they made me feel
like everything & nothing
How you made growing up existential
How one can be lulled into nostalgia
by the clamor of an audacious love.

what the fire hydrant said to the black boy

we got a tangled history the two of us
must be hard to look at me
& just see summertime
just see childhood
just see something to keep
you cool in the heat

they say we both stay posted on corners
they say we both come with warnings
for others not to stand too close
but we both mind our own business
until people use us for things
we were never meant for

do you know what it means
for your existence to be defined
by someone else's intentions?

a burning home
a burning cross
putting a boy against the wall
so the dogs
have an easier time

of course you know

a prison cell
an empty gun
a mourning mother of a boy who thought
sending him to that school across town
would mean he'd
have an easier time

but when they open us

spilling
until there's nothing left inside

everyone stands around
to watch.

Counting Descent

My grandfather is a quarter century
older than his right to vote & two
decades younger than the president
who signed the paper that made it so.

He married my grandmother when they
were four years younger than I am now
& were twice as sure about each other
as I've ever been about most things.

They had six children separated by nine
years, three cities & one Mason-Dixon
line; there were twice as many boys as girls
but half as many bedrooms as children

which most days didn't matter because poor
ain't poor unless you name it so & kids
prefer playing to counting so there was never
much time to wallow in anything but laughter.

My mother was the third oldest or the fourth
youngest depending on who you ask.
She was born on a federal holiday which my
grandmother was thankful for, said the Good

Lord only got one day off when He built
the world, so one day is all she needed too.
Mom says Pops was persistent, wouldn't give up
when he asked if he could take her down the street

to get some coffee which back then cost
two dollars less than it does now. Now
Mom is trying to stop drinking coffee but still
loves Pops, they've been married

for thirty-one years and have three kids
who are six years & 1,517 miles apart. My birth
took twelve hours, forty-three minutes
which is probably because my head

is five times too big. Mom said that my
head was big because I needed enough
room to read all the books in the library,
which seemed like infinity, even though

I didn't really know what infinity meant,
but I had heard my teacher say it once
when she talked about the universe
& books felt like the universe to me.

I was pretty good at math too, until about
fifth grade when they started putting numbers
& letters together which didn't make much sense.
My brother is seventy months younger

than me but is taller & knows more about
numbers so it doesn't always feel like this is true.
My sister is twenty-four years of loyal
& eight years of best friend. I am the oldest

of three but maybe the most naïve, I still believe
we can build this world into something new,
some place where I can live past twenty-five
& it's not a cause for celebration because these days

I celebrate every breath, tried to start counting
them so I wouldn't take each one for granted.
I wish I could give my breath to the boys who
had theirs taken, but I've stopped counting

because it feels like there are too many
boys & not enough breath to go around.

Keeping Score

The cards nestled under their noses like a magician the moment before the final act. How they abracadabra a memory out of breath. Call a spade a spade or called it a sputtering streak of light.

Pops and Uncle Craig eyed each other from across the table. Blinking like they could communicate the count in their hands through their retinas. Spades be like that. Will have grown men thinking they're X-men reincarnated at a 7th ward barbecue, like they could turn the porch into the sort of sanctuary that scoffs at what the world says they cannot do.

Mom and Auntie Ness laughed like they had nostalgia smoldering in their bellies. Heads bent backwards toward the sky as if watching constellations playing the dozens behind the moon.

You could tell they had the lead by the way Mom crossed her legs. How the crisscross of her brown beckoned for Pops' excuses, begged for him to claim she ain't do nothing but get a lucky hand. How she kept tapping the pencil on the yellow notepad the same way the rain is a metronome against concrete.

She loved to rile him up like that, turn him into the boy she met back when none of them were keeping score.

a lineage

i was named after my father   who was named after his father
who fought a war for his country   against a place he couldn't
pronounce   he held a gun   he says he never used   the gun
left his hand   but i don't think it ever left him   he came back
and cleaned carpets for white folks   then moved his family into
the same neighborhood as them   pops still remembers looking
around   and seeing no one who looked like him   most days
i look around and don't see anyone who looks   like me   most
days i am still   told i am picking up after white folks   i am trying
to disentangle my name from my grandfather's gun   i am trying
to pick it up   off the carpet and place it   back where it belongs

Counterfactual

When I was twelve years old
on a field trip some place
I can't remember, my friends
and I bought Super Soakers,

turned the hotel parking lot
into a water-filled battlezone.
We hid behind cars
running through the darkness
that lay between the streetlights.
Boundless laughter
across the pavement.

Within ten minutes
my father came outside
grabbed me by the forearm
and led me inside to our room—
his too-tight grip unfamiliar.

Before I could object,
tell him how foolish
he had made me look
in front of my friends,
he derided me for being so naïve.

Told me I couldn't be out here
acting the same as these white boys—
can't be pretending to shoot guns
can't be running in the dark
can't be hiding behind anything
other than your own teeth.

I know now how scared
he must have been,
how easily I could have fallen
into the empty of the night.
That some man would mistake
that water for a good reason
to wash all of this away.

Playground Elegy

The first time I slid down a slide my mother
　told me to hold my hands towards the sky.
　　Something about gravity, weight distribution,
　　　& feeling the air ripple through your fingers.
　　　　I reached the bottom, smile consuming half
　　　　　of my face, hands still in the air because I didn't
　　　　　　want it to stop. Ever since, this defiance of gravity
　　　　　　has always been synonymous with feeling alive.
　　　　　　　When I read of the new child, his body strewn across
　　　　　　　　the street, a casket of bones & concrete, I wonder how
　　　　　　　　many times he slid down the slide. How many times
　　　　　　　　he defied gravity to answer a question in class. Did he
　　　　　　　　　raise his hands for all of them? Does my mother regret
　　　　　　　　　　this? That she raised a black boy growing up to think that
　　　　　　　　　　raised hands made me feel more alive. That raised hands
　　　　　　　　　　meant I was alive. That raised hands meant I would live.

Ode to the Only Black Kid in the Class

You, it seems,
are the manifestation
of several lifetimes
of toil. *Brown v. Board*
in the flesh. Most days
the classroom feels
like an antechamber.
You are deemed expert
on all things Morrison,
King, Malcolm, Rosa.
Hell, weren't you sitting
on that bus, too?
You are everybody's
best friend
until you are not.
Hip-hop lyricologist.
Presumed athlete.
Free & Reduced sideshow.
Exception & caricature.
Too black & too white
all at once. If you are successful
it is because of affirmative action.
If you fail it is because
you were destined to.
You are invisible until
they turn on the Friday
night lights. Here you are—
star before they render
you asteroid. Before they
watch you turn to dust.

what the window said to the black boy

when someone breaks me they call it a crime
they call it property damage
they call it the breaking the social contract

when someone breaks you they call it inevitable
they call it your fault
they call it wednesday

they say that it's you who came cracked
came shattered right out the box
but they don't know that this is just something you do

to show how many of you there are
that none of you are the same
that the more shards there are

the more ways there are
to refract this light
that envelops us each day

Saturday Morning Routine

Mom poured the flour straight from the bag,
milk straight from the carton.
You can't measure things you just know.

I was never much of a cook.
My job was to clean up after,
wipe everything away and leave

the counter pristine
so she could eat breakfast
with her nerves calm.

I still have a habit of trying to make up
for things I can't understand
by removing all of the evidence.

When Maze & Frankie Beverly Come on in My House

Mom's eyes close.
She raises the spatula
as if she were going to orchestrate
the gumbo into existence.
Turns the knob so that we feel
the bass thundering in the walls.

At the start of verse one,
        she points to Pops,
        walks over, shoulders
        oscillating back-and-forth
        between the melody.
        Pops does the same dance
        he's been doing since '73—
        left knee, right knee, pop, snap
        left knee, right knee, pop, snap.

At the start of verse two,
        Pops drops his shoulder,
        bites his bottom lip,
        & does some sort of spin move
        pivoting on his left foot.
        When he does this it's unclear
        if he's hurt his back
        or if he's doing an unauthorized
        version of the sprinkler.
        The way his hands flip & turn
        & slap box the sky between them.
        The way Mom looks confused
        as to what exactly is happening
        but she goes with it, 'cuz she's fly
        like that & has never left Pops
        hanging on the dance floor.

At the start of verse three,
        smoke alarms are going off
        in the kitchen.
        Their hands are clasped
        now, fingers interlocked,

swinging each other back & forth.
Their feet are now music
of their own.

At the end of the song,
           Frankie's voice begins to fade
           but they keep dancing. She holds
           her hand on the back of his neck,
           he pulls her in closer, she looks
           at him, kisses him between the sweat
           rolling down his forehead.
           Then they laugh
           & laugh & laugh & laugh
           long after the song has stopped.

Ode to the Drizzy Drake Hands

I see how you operate.
Traversing through the air
as if unbounded by space and time.
The rest of us can only hope for
an agency as unapologetic as yours.
You are jazz hands falling into
evolution, cross-continental
symbol of unrestrained ecstasy.
You are our favorite
cultural phenomenon.
Have been turned into puns
that wander the undercurrents
of the Internet. They try to make
you a jester of squandered masculinity,
but you were never here for that.
This was always about the music.
This was always about how you
could turn a house party into a time
capsule. This was always about how
music just ain't music if it don't make
your fingers shake a little bit.
This was always about how a group
of people you love all dancing in one
room can make your chest rumble
with something you almost forgot you had.

How to Fight

My favorite part of class
was always the spelling bee.
One by one children would
slip on syllables until there
were only a few of us left.

We weren't allowed to write
anything down as we stood
in front of the class, so I used
my fingers to trace an outline
in the air of words Mrs. Roberts
read from her blue dictionary.

We didn't say certain words in
my home because we were told
they could hurt people,
but words were the only
way I ever knew how to fight.

Spelling bees were a battleground
where teachers trained me
to wield language as a
tool & fist & weapon & warning
to those who would rather
make an outline out of me.

Zero Gravity

At my cousin's seventh birthday party the space walk
becomes the celestial body around which all of us orbit.
I marvel at the way it merges the cosmic & the terrestrial.
How the inner walls are lined with the frosting from fingers
that do not believe in false dichotomies, do not believe
in the choice between a plate of cake & defying gravity.
I volunteer to serve as chaperone inside this earthbound
chamber of physics. What is the general theory of relatively
when buoyed by the laughter of twelve seven-year-olds?
Let us marvel at the way they turn a body into a satellite
to amplify their bliss. Let us praise the bare feet
that serve as launch-pad to all we have yet to see.

Ode to the End-of-Year 6th Grade Picnic

It began with a game of two-hand touch, though such
administratively imposed regulations were quickly
forgotten as soon as the Isley Brothers record started
playing and the teachers two-stepped off into the distance.

Coach Lonnie turned toward the grill, spatula in hand,
ready to turn burgers into reprieve from subpar report
cards. We just called him Coach, although his large belly
belied the athletic prowess of his past. He flipped his

fleur-de-lis cap backwards and threw on an apron
that read, *Always something good cookin' in my kitchen.*
I had just learned how to spell *innuendo* though I still
wasn't sure what it meant. Later, The Hot Boys

were blasting through large Sony speakers that turned
everywhere within a 200-foot radius into unrepentant
celebration. Lil' Wayne assuring us with brazen certainty
that the block indeed was hot, as even the most secure

of us heeded the warning to check the underside
of our feet. Ensuring the safety of our appendages,
we returned to the feast. Hot dog in one hand,
Kool-Aid in the other, all of us singularly committed

to getting our roll on. The girls danced in clusters,
becoming accustomed to the bourgeoning parabola
of their hips, learning the power they wielded over boys
who were dawdling amalgamations of awkward

and bravado. Prepubescent pick-up lines made
rejection quotidian and gave your boys ammunition
for weeks to come. Each crack helping us learn to love
the sound of one another's laughter.

Passed Down

Sometimes I forget there are freckles
on my face. It's the sort of thing where

I'm not always proud of my skin
for being light enough to illuminate the patches

of darkness that emerge from beneath it.
A colony of inconsistent color

spread out across this countenance. The remnants
of colonialism in this double-helix

of a body. When I was younger I was ashamed
of my mother for the heirloom

of her cheeks, always wondering why she
couldn't just keep them to herself.

Dissection

The day John F. Kennedy was killed
my grandfather was in the lab.
He was a zoologist, made a living
from looking at the dead.
Took animals apart to understand
what made them whole.

He would sit the radio
between test tubes & Bunsen burners.
A safe haven of sorts.

The President has been shot.

The beaker slipped from the tongs,
a mosaic of shattered glass.
He couldn't remember the sound

of glass breaking, only the hum
of the radio whittling the country
to its knees.

He turned knobs until the room echoed
into silence.
Grabbed his jacket

went home to his wife.
The bloodied carcass still left
for all to see.

On January 8, 1811 Charles Deslondes, a mixed race slave driver, led what would become the largest slave revolt in American History, rallying an army of five hundred slaves outside of New Orleans to fight for freedom.

For Charles

Charles, I imagine there came a point
where you decided enough was enough,
the sound of cowhide against flesh,

the alchemy of blood and sweat sitting
atop your lip, how the wind
from the Mississippi cooled the skin

when it raced across your mouth, teasing
your tongue to follow it beyond this
place. Or maybe they called you *boy*

one time too many; emasculated you
in front those you held dear. Or maybe
you grew weary of holding the whip

in your own hand, realized they had made
you a proxy for their deeds. When you
and the others came together to plan

the inevitable, hurled whispers from plantation
to plantation—a clarion call of what could
no longer wait—had you already accepted

what would be made of you? Did you anticipate
how they would slice your hands at the wrist?
Render your femurs two shattered vases. Burn

you at the stake while you watched them behead
the others, pull the intestines through
their mouths and wrap them around the bodies.

One traveler wrote: *Their heads, which decorate*
our levee, all the way up the coast, look like crows
sitting on long poles. Could you have known

that they would make a scarecrow of you?
I grew up hearing these stories, of heads jettisoned
from the body and mounted above the streetlights

for everyone to see. Charles, they may leave me
roasting in the sun as well, a warning that the sweet
whisper of the Mississippi must persist.

For the Boys Who Never Learned How to Swim

The police sirens sounded like wind
getting knocked out of our stomachs.
We tried to find a place to pull over

where there was a semblance of light.
There was no light.
They asked us to step out of the car.

I didn't know why—they grabbed him
like he wasn't somebody's child,
palmed the back of his head

like soft fruit ready to be dropped
from the top of the roof so everyone
could laugh at the plurality of pieces.

His face against the front of the police
car made him look like a fish out of water.

> *But where is the water?*
> *When has there ever been water?*
> *When have we ever been allowed to swim?*
> *When has there ever been somewhere*
> *we can breathe?*

I don't remember the last time police
sirens didn't feel like gasping for air.
I don't remember what it means not

to be considered something meant
to flounder, to flap against
the surface while others watch you

until the flailing   stops.

Beyond This Place

The air is thick with ambivalence, the residue of those both forgotten and pushed away. There is a watchtower too certain of its own authority. The slow grating of a mechanical door grants one passage in and out of the yard. The dull gray of clothing renders life invisible against a backdrop of concrete walls. Barbed wire coils itself precariously around the edges of asphalt. It can be difficult to tell what they are trying to keep in and what they are trying to keep out. Chain link fences stand upright as soldiers do—they do only what they are told, only what they have convinced themselves they have been built for.

But is anything built for what it ultimately becomes? When this steel was melded into a false deity, a pretense of human control, did it dream of what else it could have been? The wheels of a child's first bicycle? The monkey bars from which they would swing to and fro? The car a family drives on cross-country road trip filled with laughter and fighting and spilled ketchup across the floor? When did it learn it was to become a cage? What is a cage beyond that which it holds?

Lance is made of heavy bones and inquisition. He is a soft barrage of endless questions yet judicious with his words. Tyrus is broad shoulders and calm eyes, elegant dreadlocks falling along his back. Leo is a linebacker swallowed by a young child's laugh, his porcelain head reflecting the incandescent light from above. Chad is a thick New England accent imbued with Boston bravado. His wide-framed glasses consume half of his small face. Darryl is a long salt-and-pepper goatee that curls back beneath the underside of his chin, he is the gravity that pulls us all closer to the center.

It is a classroom of men who refuse to forget themselves, each word provides the sort of freedom a parole board can never grant. They write about their families, their children. Wanting them to remember their father as the man whose laugh would turn a room into a festival of rapture, someone who would read them stories before they fell asleep to a world that didn't always make sense, but always made sense in his arms. They want people to remember that they once existed beyond this place, that they still do.

For the Taxi Cabs that Pass Me in Harvard Square

When the first cab passes you,
    wonder if you've been rendered
    an autumn tree, derelict
    monument amid the white noise
    of Massachusetts Ave.

When the second cab passes you,
    pull off your hood & hat
    even though the ice is fresh.
    You don't want to be mistaken
    for a shadow, a threat.

When the third cab passes you,
    pull out your Ivy League ID,
    & wave it in your hand
    like the curb was a desert island.

When the fourth cab passes you,
    think of 5th grade. Mrs. Capperson holding
    all the boys in for recess to tell us if we don't
    get tattoos, grow out our hair, pierce our ears,
    or sag our pants everything will be all right.

When the fifth cab passes you,
    know everything is not all right.

When the sixth cab passes you,
    imagine yourself a puddle
    existing as both transparency
    & filth. Something that won't be there
    by the afternoon.

When the seventh cab passes you,
    remember how Grandma said this is how
    long it took for the Good Lord to build
    the world.

James Baldwin Speaks to the Protest Novel

I admire what you're seeking to do, my friend. I, too, have dreamt the possibilities of this pen. I have held onto it so long that is has become a proxy for these fingers, which is to say all that allows me to hold onto things, which is to say I have never been good at holding on to things. It's just that you make a caricature of my mother, my brother, the vitality of my nephew's laugh. They are swallowed inside of you. Each of them becomes a pawn to your politics, a bullet used in ideological warfare that cannot be won like this. It is not your job to prove a point here, to make a statement other than that there can be life amid these pages. Is Bigger Thomas nothing more than a tempest awaiting to erupt? Is Miss Ophelia merely a white knight adorned in ink? To deny the full humanity of others is to deny it within ourselves. I want to see all of the complexity and mess and joy and distress of being a complex human being, which is to say a human being. Because isn't this the problem? That we must write the most exaggerated versions of ourselves to show them something they have already chosen not to see? How can they think us more human if we don't write ourselves as such?

Canon

Our stars weren't meant for
their sky. We have never known
the same horizon.

On Observing My Home After the Storm

I.

The smell
                              so pungent you can see it,
          the fermentation of sky
                         prickling at your skin.
                    An alloy of brackish & sewer water
stinging nostrils, the residue of cries
                         for help.
                              Eyes unprepared for this
sort of wreckage.
                    The maggots demarcate the space
between what was & never will be
                    again.
                              Steel door hinges split at the seam.
          Every wall, a groundswell of lusterless green.
Glass has meandered
               across the floor,
                              a cacophony of shattered skin.
                    The overturned dinner table
          sits on its side
                         as if to protect the rest of the house
from the night it knows will come.
                    The floorboards do not creak,
                              they whimper—
          distraught by all they could not prevent.

II.

But what are these words
but an empty lyric?
What then is anything,
beyond the language we give it?
What else do we have
to describe the carnage we see
but all that is woefully inadequate?

what is left

how warm did the water have to be   before it gave the sky permission
to crumble   when the levees broke open   did the ocean intend
to swallow the city   or find refuge inside of it   is it wrong to love
something more   after it has already disappeared   is it still called
disappearing   if no one knew you were there   the scientist tells me
that we have been disappearing for a long time now   the evangelist
tells me   this is what happens   when you make a mockery of time
the television tells me   this is really the best thing that could have
happened   to a burning city   my mother was born in a city   that
is asking how this happened   i was born in a city   that knows how
this happened   i was born in the same city as my mother   i was born
in this city   which i am told makes it mine   my father was not born
in this city   but has lived here longer   than I have been alive   can
you claim something as your own   if you don't remember how
you found it   i come from a city that is drowning   while being told
it is rinsing itself clean

Lifeline

my city sustains itself by hosting
those who will not stay

they eat, they drink
they laugh, they dance
they buy, they spend
they come, they go

to survive
we need the money
of those who do not care
who we have been
but only what we offer
it's not that i'm resentful
it's just that we are addicted
to what always leaves us

The Protest Novel Responds to James Baldwin

You misunderstand me, James. This isn't for them. This is for you, for us. This here is catharsis. You are right that I have a point to make. Miss Ophelia wasn't written to show white folks who they are but to show them who they need to be. Bigger Thomas wasn't made to suggest that we aren't more than this anger, he was written for our boys to know they're not alone in feeling it. This is a protest against isolation, against loneliness, against thinking you're the only one experiencing the trauma that leaves a man full of cracks. Didn't you say that, James? That books showed you that you weren't alone in your pain? You talk about humanity, but what is more human than seeing yourself in another? I remember when holding me would have gotten you killed. Now you pen these pages yourself. Is that not a protest, James? Is that not resisting all that they never meant for us to do? We've got to protest on these pages. This ink be our picket line. How can we write about the soil and not talk about the blood? How can we write about the tree and not talk about the noose? Ain't no *ars poetica* here, James. This here is for our survival.

The Men in Orange

The first time you step in a prison

will be for your orientation as a new

writing instructor at the correctional

center. They won't let you go beyond

the first room because your paper-

work has not processed. The room

smells like a place where few things

pass in & out; it will linger on

your tongue long after you depart. It

tastes like the time you were a boy

& saw all of those men in orange picking

up trash along the street, a man in blue

watching them from atop a horse. How

they kept the roads clean but the whole

thing made you feel like dirt. How the

man on top of the horse looked like he

thought he belonged there, like he deserved

praise for keeping everything in order.

How Malcolm Learned to Read

Malcolm copied every word from the dictionary
when he was locked away in prison. Spent every
night in the corner of his cell, a glowing asylum
where the corridor light squeezed its way past
the guards like a disobedient child. His eyes
darting back and forth between each page, tracing
the wisps of fleeting letters with dwindling lead
staining his thumb. The first page took him all night.
He spent the next day trying to anchor each syllable
to his memory's harbor before it was drawn away.

I'd written words that I never knew were in the world.

Malcolm, I, too, have tried to inscribe my way
to something new. Have tried to use writing as a way
to leave behind the man I wasn't proud to be.
Now, sometimes it feels like these words are all I have.
Sometimes I forget who I was before these words,
before these stages, before the applause from strangers,
before being asked what I thought about things I didn't know.
Malcolm, could you have ever imagined
what this dictionary would make of you? Do you
remember who you were before you picked up the pen?

From the Cell Block

Daniel has been in prison
since he was seventeen.
He has woken up every day
for the past thirty-eight years to
a cell block and diminishing
sense of what existed before.
On some days, he says,
he wakes up, looks
outside his window and misses
being able to see the trees,
how they change colors at the end
of September, how they fall
from each branch and litter
the ground like the dust
of secondhand stars. How he can
still hear them, the sound of
leaves skipping atop the concrete
on the other side of the wall.

How to Make an Empty Cardboard Box Disappear in 10 Steps

1) Find the scissors
2) Cut the sides of the cube
3) Attend the rally of Trayvon Martin
4) Attend the rally of Renisha McBride
5) Attend the rally of Jordan Davis
6) Attend the rally of Michael Brown
7) Attend the rally of Eric Garner
8) Attend the rally of Freddie Gray
9) Find another empty box
10) Attend the rally of _____

Meteor Shower

I read somewhere that meteor showers
are almost always named after

the constellation from which
they originate. It's funny, I think,

how even the universe is telling us
that we can never get too far

from the place that created us.
How there is always a streak of our past

trailing closely behind us
like a smattering of obstinate memories.

Even when we enter a new atmosphere,
become subsumed in flames, turn to dust,

lose ourselves in the wind, and scatter
the surface of all that rests beneath us,

we bring a part of where we are from
to every place we go.

Chaos Theory

If twenty million years ago
the butterfly flew in a different
direction do you think
we would have met, maybe
we wouldn't have even been
people, maybe we wouldn't
have even been us, you know,
maybe you would have
been a tortoise and I would
be a raspberry,
maybe we would both be plants
on opposite sides of the same
coral reef, so that we could
have been connected without
ever having met,
maybe I would be an oak cut
down to be the home that held
you, maybe I would have never
been, maybe the butterfly's wings
would have blown the seed
into the river
and away from the soil
which otherwise would have
become a bush of blueberries
which otherwise would have
been eaten by a squirrel or
some other prehistoric rodent
which otherwise
would have died
in a field of milkweeds
which otherwise would have
been carried by the wind
to another place
which otherwise might have
gotten caught in the feathers
of the bird which otherwise
might have flown to the other
side of the sea I could go on

but what I mean to say
is that it would have been
such a tragedy
if something happened
that would have prevented me
from meeting you
like a butterfly
who didn't realize it was flying
in the wrong direction.

No More Elegies Today

Today I will
write a poem
about a little girl jumping rope.
It will not be a metaphor
for dodging bullets.
It will not be an allegory
for skipping past despair.
But rather about the
back & forth bob of her head
as she waits for the right moment
to insert herself
into the blinking flashes
of bound hemp.
But rather about her friends
on either end of the rope who turn
their wrists into small
flashing windmills cultivating
an energy of their own.
But rather about the way
the beads in her hair bounce
against the back of her neck.
But rather the way her feet
barely touch the ground,
how the rope skipping across
the concrete sounds
like the entire world is giving
her a round of applause.

An Evening at the Louvre

Who could have imagined
it would be like this
not possibly the Greek sculptor
who chiseled the block
of marble into an impossibly
beautiful thing
now the selfie-sticks surround
the statue like a barricade
of tightly knit smiles
or the ever-changing tentacles
of an octopus which is ironic
for a statue made famous
by its absence of appendages
the Louvre is an impossibly
large museum with an impossibly
beautiful pyramid of glass
protruding from beneath the surface
you tell me how cute you think
I look with my audio guide
dangling from my neck
these headphones which must be
from 1997 sitting atop my head
you are impossibly beautiful
and sometimes I look at you
when I should be looking
at these remnants of antiquity
sometimes I want to sculpt you
but I could never do justice
to your eyes
besides why waste time sculpting
when I could make you pancakes
in the morning
while you're still sleeping
your feet poking out from under
the sheets but maybe I am getting
ahead of myself because right now
we are in the Louvre and the audio
guide is telling me how so much
of archeology is conjecture
which is to say just a guess

I wonder how many things
the world has deemed fact
that are actually just presumptions
made by men in robes or glasses
or scrolls full of poems like this one
I have lots of ideas but I'm not sure
if any are right
it would be nice to be
something in a museum one day
because that's what I've been told
means you've lived a meaningful life
but I think instead I might like
to be in a garden
where even after I die the residue
of me can help grow something
more beautiful than I ever was

An Inquiry

Your mother came to this country
folded inside her own echo.
She crossed an ocean,
left one pocket of earth
for another.
She still holds her tongue
over two coasts.
All I have of war are questions,
never answers.
How might we begin
to unravel a shadow?
How many bullets
can one see before nostalgia
no longer covers the wounds?
Is it possible to misremember
what the dust in a collapsing stomach
tastes like?
When a dead child's blood dries
on your hands does it convince your skin
to scar? I want to ask her
how many layers there are to fear
that she can no longer see.

Each Morning Is a Ritual Made Just for Us

you wake up first on the left side of the bed, kiss my cheek and let your feet slide onto the coolness of the wooden floor, which sometimes creeks depending on the how cold the weather is but it is the beginning of autumn so today it is soft like a distant whistle, just like we were eight years old and this was the end of recess but really you and I have never stopped playing, and I feel like that's what makes this so great, we laugh as often as we breathe, but I apologize if I'm getting off topic, this is supposed to be a poem about how I listen to you pitter-patter across the room as the sun rises and I still pretend to be asleep, my eyes shut while I hear the splashing of water against skin from the bathroom, and these are the moments when I feel most lucky, when the steam is sliding out from behind the door and you emerge looking like everything that has ever mattered and I can't pretend to be asleep anymore because how could I keep lying about how remarkable it is to get to see you each day before the rest of the world does, now by this time I have gotten out of bed and started looking for the iron which I can somehow never seem to find and it's not like I need it anyway, it's not like my pants are that wrinkly, but sometimes routine feels nice because it is familiar and you are something I hope remains familiar for as long as I keep waking up each morning you know these mornings full of NPR and exercises we're a bit too tired to do, but we do it anyway because one day we'll have kids and hopefully they'll have kids and we want to be healthy enough to run around in the park with them while they ask us questions about how plants grow and why dogs seem like they can run forever, I know I keep talking about forever but it's hard when that's all I see in the mornings when you kiss me and pitter-patter across the floor while I pretend to be asleep

Line/Breaks

In their song,
"Last Days Reloaded,"
when Dead Prez said,
taking my own life/
into my own hands
it was the first time I
understood line breaks.
It wasn't *The Odyssey*.
It wasn't *Hamlet*.
It was when stic.man told me
how the police had made
a mockery of his home.
Mrs. Johnson had never
spoken of it this way
when she explained
it at the board,
how you could capture
disillusion & agency
in the span of one breath,
this duplicity of danger,
this split tongue.
This language that cannot be
contained by a single

                    space.

When They Tell You the Brontosaurus Never Existed

you will wonder what kind of precedent we are setting here.
The placemats that sat under uneaten broccoli delineating
the Jurassic as a place plentiful with baby Brontosaurus?

Utter fabrication.

The Land Before Time—I through XIII?

All a lie.

The Flintstones' tales of Brontosaurus Burgers galore?

Mere fiction.

You will wave goodbye as this dinosaur joins Pluto, drifting off
into the purgatory of things that once were. You will wonder
what it means to have spent your entire life being taught
something is real, only to be told it was all an accident.

The wrong skull, they say.
150 million years of mistake.
How often are we given this message?
That everything would have been fine if you only had a different face?
A different head

on your shoulders. What is existence really
if its definition is so ephemeral—if all that history
can be snatched away?

Today I Bought a Book for You

it wasn't one I had ever heard of
but the first page had your favorite word

and that was enough for me
to unfold the dollar bills from my pockets.

I remember the first time
you told me what it meant.

I wrote it down in my notebook
with the hopes of using it later

to impress you.
I have a notebook full of these.

It should come as no surprise.
I have always used words

to try and convince the world
that I am worth something.

Shout Out

Shout out to the light of the city
      for deafening the stars

Shout out to the splintering floorboard
      for announcing my entrance to every room

Shout out to the curtain over the window
      for swallowing the sun

Shout out to the internment thunderstorms
      for holding the city hostage

Shout out to the engine of the car
      for eroding away the night

Shout out to the chalk on the blackboard
      for leaving its shadow behind

Shout out to the shade over the lamp
      for providing respite for the moon

Shout out to the tide of the ocean
      for erasing the residue of time

Shout out to the 9pm train
      for becoming the catacomb of another day

Shout out to the copper statue after the rain
      for being a paragon of transformation

Shout out to the horizon
      for disguising our grief so beautifully

Shout out to the branches of the oak tree
      for re-inscribing the sky

It Is Early December in Cambridge

and the Charles River has crystallized into a
glimmering pane of fresh glass. Not yet strong
enough to stand on but beautiful enough
to watch from the bridge above. The bridge,
its subtle arc, encrusted in an overlay of white,
a small child dawdling across with adult in hand,
little joints fixed in place by the four layers of
clothes on her body, a swaddle of stiff limbs.
When she first sees the snow, she becomes
overwhelmed with joy, slips away to chase the
bits of sky, tottering a few feet before tumbling
under the weight of her own elation. She rolls,
her small body becoming an avalanche unto
itself, squeals of laughter growing with each
rotation. I watch the woman, her mother
perhaps, dart anxiously after the rolling bundle
checking for cuts, scratches, bruises, signs of
distress. But the child is still laughing, undeterred
by blood. Gets back on her feet, waiting for
the next slice of sky worth chasing.

When Mom Braids My Sister's Hair

Oprah usually plays on the TV in the background. Jess sits crisscross applesauce in front of the couch, Mom sitting above her, legs wrapped around either side of my small sister's trembling frame, her hair two hemispheres of Afro puff, a vertical equator of scalp running its way onto the unseen side of her head. Two minutes in, and tears are already streaking down her face, each circumnavigating freckles before falling to the carpet below. The comb is a contestation of plastic and naps, hair as uncooperative as it is remarkable. Jess keeps crying and Mom despairs over the heaving child, *You're just as tender-headed as your Auntie was*. Mom wipes the wetness from her face, leans over to kiss her forehead and stroke the nape of her neck. Jess' sobbing slows, and she smiles as Oprah gives a woman a new house or a new car or some other shiny thing. Mom grabs three pieces of hair, uses the magician in her fingers to slip the strands between one another. She asks me to go stir the beans on the stove, the crackling of the comb between hair indistinguishable from the gas fire brewing beneath our Sunday dinner. I step onto the kitchen stool and move the spoon slowly inside the pot, peeking over the counter to watch the procession of thumbs and tresses continue, unsure how such transformation is possible. *Alright, you're done*. Jess hops up from the carpet and runs to the mirror beaming as if the pain was never there. Her new braids swinging from her head, a wreath of calla lilies in the wind.

For the Hardest Days

Some evenings, after days when the world feels
like it has poured all of its despair onto me,
when I am awash with burdens that rests atop
my body like a burlap of jostling shadows,

I find a place to watch the sun set. I dig
my feet into a soil that has rebirthed itself
a millions times over. I listen to the sound
of leaves as they decide whether or not

it is time to descend from their branches.
It is hard to describe the comfort one feels
in sitting with something you trust will always be
there, something you can count on to remain

familiar when all else seems awry. How remarkable
it is to know that so many have watched the same
sun set before you. How the wind can carry
pollen and drop it somewhere it has never been.
How the leaves have always become the soil

that then become the leaves again. How maybe
we are not so different from the leaves.
How maybe we are also always being reborn
to be something more then we once were.

How maybe that's what waking up each morning is.
A reminder that we are born
of the same atoms as every plant and bird
and mountain and ocean around us.

Queries of Unrest

Maybe I come from the gap
between my father's teeth.
Maybe I was meant to see a little
bit of darkness every time he smiled.

Maybe I was meant to understand that
darkness magnifies the sight of joy.
Maybe I come from where the sidewalk
ends, or maybe I just read that in a book once.
It can be hard to tell the difference sometimes.

Maybe when I was a kid
a white boy told me I was marginalized
and all I could think of was the edge
of a sheet of paper, how empty it is—
the abyss I was told never to write into.

Maybe I'm scared of writing another poem
that makes people roll their eyes
and say, "another black poem."
Maybe I'm scared people won't think
of the poem as a poem, but as a cry for help.

Maybe the poem is a cry for help.

Maybe I come from a place
where people are always afraid of dying.
Maybe that's just what I tell myself
so I don't feel so alone in this body.
Maybe there's a place where everyone is both
in love with and running from their own skin.
Maybe that place is here.

Maybe that's why I'm always running
from the things that love me. Maybe I'm trying
to save them the time of burying darkness
when all they have to do is close their eyes.

what the cathedral said to the black boy

come inside child
rest yourself
it's okay to want to be held
ain't we all just trying to be
some type of sanctuary for someone?
for every year we are not destroyed
do they not remind us what a miracle
it is to have lasted this long?
amid this plunder
amid all this wreckage
take a breath and call it prayer
take a step and call living
what that ocean tell you child?
that they're frightened of you?
they fear you because they ain't
ready for your type of holy
close your eyes
those stained glass shadows
all we got is what we name ourselves
otherwise I am just a room
you are just body
& we know how wrong that is

There is a Lake Here

For New Orleans

There is a lake here.
A lake the size of
outstretched arms. And no,
not the type of arms raised
in surrender. I mean the sort
of arms beckoning to be held.
To wrap themselves around another
and to never let go. And no, the lake
is not a place where people are
drowning. And no, this water is not
that which comes from a storm
or that which turns a city
into a tessellation of broken
windows and spray paint.
There are children swimming here,
splashing one another while
the droplets ricochet between them.
The droplets do not hurt,
they simply roll down the side
of the boy's cheek. No, the boy is not
using the water to hide his tears.
He is laughing. Eyes cast out across
the water, in awe of how vast it is.

Notes

a lineage is written after Safia Elhillo

Counterfactual is an excerpt from Clint's 2015 TED Talk "How to Raise a Black Son in America"

Counting Descent is written after Alan Michael Parker

James Baldwin Speaks to the Protest Novel is written after and borrowing from James Baldwin

Keeping Score is written after Nabila Lovelace

Meteor Shower is written after Adam Scheffler

Queries of Unrest is written after Hanif Willis-Abdurraqib

Something You Should Know is written after Ross Gay

The first line of *Shout Out* is borrowed from Adam Scheffler

There is a Lake Here is written after Jamaal May

Acknowledgements

Write Bloody, thank you for believing in this book.

Mom and Dad, thank you for keeping me safe, for loving me hard, and for always reminding me how big the world is. Jess and Tal, you all are with me in everything I do, you always have been. Auntie, thank you for always looking out for me. Thank you to my grandparents, who created the path.

Gavin, none of this is possible without you. You showed me the way.

Mahogany Browne, as you have done for so many, you and the Nuyorican Poets Café were the first place to show me I had a voice that could be heard.

Elizabeth Acevedo, Pages Matam, Amin Dallal, Terisa Siagotonu, George Yamazawa you are my partners in this journey unlike any others.

Alan Michael Parker, Gregory Pardlo, Vievee Francis, Brenda Flanagan, Jorie Graham, and Cathy Hightower thank you for being remarkable teachers. Your passion and thoughtfulness recommitted me to the craft.

Thank you to those who, in so many ways, have contributed to this project with your eyes, your words, or your encouragement over the years: Sarah Kay, Hanif Willis-Abdurraqib, Eve Ewing, Nabila Lovelace, Anis Mojgani, Kiese Laymon, Amanda Torres, Sterling Higa, Darrell Scott, Marc Bacani, Mark Jimenez, Matthew Clair, Ebony Chinn, Diamond Forde, Yolanda Franklin, Charleen Mcclure, Jessica Lanay Moore, Jennifer Steele, Najee Omar, Mckendy Fils-Aimé, Sarah Lawson, Safia Elhillo, Anthony Febo, Jason Henry Simon-Bierenbaum, Chris August, Kane Smego, Matt Gallant, Twain Dooley, Joseph Green, Gail Danley, Brandon Douglas, Roscoe Burnems, Robalu Gibsun, Adele Hampton, Natalie Illum, Jusna Perrin, Gowri Koneswaran, Jonathan Tucker, Drew Anderson, Dwayne Lawson-Brown, Sarah Browning, Angelique Palmer, Katy Richey, Venessa Marco, Alysia Harris, Diamond Sharp, Neville Adams, Sonya Renee Taylor, Rasheed Copeland, Adam Scheffler, Michael Lee, Donald Mokgale, Lily Million, Lazarus Mathebula, Shihan Van Clief, Javon Johnson, Carlos Robson, Mike Simms, Juwan

Blocker, Joshua Abah, Cici Felton, Mariana Sheppard, Tarriona Tank Ball, Sha'Condria Sibley, Akeem Martin, Kataalyst Alcindor, Justin Lamb, Sam Gordon, Mwende Katwiwa, Denice Frohman, Malachi Byrd, Thomas Hill, Porsha Olayiwola, Janae Johnson, the FreeWord poets of Davidson College, Cave Canem, the Callaloo Creative Writing Workshop, the National Science Foundation, The Beltway Poetry Slam, Busboys and Poets, Spit Dat, Harvard University, the men at Bay State Correctional Center and MCI-Norfolk, my students at Parkdale High School, and so many others.

Ariel, you make me a fuller version of myself. I can never adequately express my gratitude for all that you have brought to my life.

Thank you to the following journals and anthologies who have published versions of poems from this book, sometimes under different names:

American Literary Review, "For Charles" & "How to Make an Empty Cardboard Box Disappear in 10 Steps

Bat City Review, "For the Taxi Cabs that Pass me in Harvard Square"

Bird's Thumb, "Ode to the Loop-de-Loop" & "Line/Breaks"

Drunk in a Midnight Choir, "Ode to 9th & O NW," "When Maze & Frankie Beverly Come on in my House," & "a lineage"

Kinfolks Quarterly, "Counting Descent"

Lime Hawk, "what the ocean said to the black boy"

Mason's Road, "Soles"

Off the Coast, "what the cicada said to the black boy"

Public Pool, "Full-Court Press," "My Jump Shot," & "How to Fight"

Still: The Journal, "Playground Elegy" & "Counterfactual"

Switchback, "Keeping Score"

The Diverse Arts Project, "Meteor Shower"

The Fire This Time Anthology - Scribner Books, "Queries of Unrest"

Watershed Review, "Ode to the Only Black Kid in the Class"

Waypoints Magazine, "Ode to the End-of-6th Grade Picnic"

Winter Tangerine Review, "For the Boys Who Never Learned How to Swim"

Photo by Clarence Maurice

CLINT SMITH is a doctoral candidate at Harvard University and has received fellowships from Cave Canem, the Callaloo Creative Writing Workshop, and the National Science Foundation. He is a 2014 National Poetry Slam champion and was a speaker at the 2015 TED Conference. His writing has been published in *The New Yorker, The Guardian, The American Literary Review, Boston Review, Harvard Educational Review* and elsewhere. He was born and raised in New Orleans.

www.clintsmithiii.com
Twitter: @ClintSmithIII
Facebook: www.facebook.com/clintsmithiii

IF YOU LIKE CLINT SMITH, CLINT SMITH LIKES...

The Pocketknife Bible
Anis Mojgani

Floating, Brilliant, Gone
Franny Choi

as well as works by Sarah Kay, Pages Matam, and Aaron Samuels.

Write Bloody Publishing distributes and promotes great books of fiction, poetry and art every year. We are an independent press dedicated to quality literature and book design, with an office in Los Angeles, CA.

Our employees are authors and artists so we call ourselves a family. Our design team comes from all over America: modern painters, photographers and rock album designers create book covers we're proud to be judged by.

We publish and promote 8-12 tour-savvy authors per year. We are grass-roots, D.I.Y., bootstrap believers. Pull up a good book and join the family. Support independent authors, artists and presses.

**Want to know more about Write Bloody books, authors and events?
Join our maling list at**

www.writebloody.com

WRITE BLOODY BOOKS

After the Witch Hunt — **Megan Falley**

Aim for the Head: An Anthology of Zombie Poetry — **Rob Sturma, Editor**

Amulet — **Jason Bayani**

Any Psalm You Want — **Khary Jackson**

Birthday Girl with Possum — **Brendan Constantine**

The Bones Below — **Sierra DeMulder**

Born in the Year of the Butterfly Knife — **Derrick C. Brown**

Bring Down the Chandeliers — **Tara Hardy**

Ceremony for the Choking Ghost — **Karen Finneyfrock**

Courage: Daring Poems for Gutsy Girls — **Karen Finneyfrock, Mindy Nettifee & Rachel McKibbens, Editors**

Dear Future Boyfriend — **Cristin O'Keefe Aptowicz**

Dive: The Life and Fight of Reba Tutt — **Hannah Safren**

Drunks and Other Poems of Recovery — **Jack McCarthy**

The Elephant Engine High Dive Revival **anthology**

Everything Is Everything — **Cristin O'Keefe Aptowicz**

The Feather Room — **Anis Mojgani**

Gentleman Practice — **Buddy Wakefield**

Glitter in the Blood: A Guide to Braver Writing — **Mindy Nettifee**

Good Grief — **Stevie Edwards**

The Good Things About America — **Derrick Brown & Kevin Staniec, Editors**

Hot Teen Slut — **Cristin O'Keefe Aptowicz**

I Love Science! — **Shanny Jean Maney**

I Love You Is Back — **Derrick C. Brown**

The Importance of Being Ernest — **Ernest Cline**

In Search of Midnight — **Mike McGee**

The Incredible Sestina Anthology — **Daniel Nester, Editor**

Junkyard Ghost Revival **anthology**

Kissing Oscar Wilde — **Jade Sylvan**

The Last Time as We Are — **Taylor Mali**

Learn Then Burn — **Tim Stafford & Derrick C. Brown, Editors**

Learn Then Burn Teacher's Manual — **Tim Stafford & Molly Meacham, Editors**

Live for a Living — **Buddy Wakefield**

Love in a Time of Robot Apocalypse — **David Perez**

The Madness Vase — **Andrea Gibson**

The New Clean — **Jon Sands**

New Shoes on a Dead Horse — **Sierra DeMulder**

No Matter the Wreckage — **Sarah Kay**

Oh, Terrible Youth — **Cristin O'Keefe Aptowicz**

The Oregon Trail Is the Oregon Trail — **Gregory Sherl**

Over the Anvil We Stretch — **Anis Mojgani**

The Pocket Knife Bible — Anis Mojgani

Pole Dancing to Gospel Hymns — **Andrea Gibson**

Racing Hummingbirds — **Jeanann Verlee**

Redhead and the Slaughter King — Megan Falley

Rise of the Trust Fall — **Mindy Nettifee**

Said the Manic to the Muse — Jeananne Verlee

Scandalabra — **Derrick C. Brown**

Slow Dance with Sasquatch — **Jeremy Radin**

The Smell of Good Mud — **Lauren Zuniga**

Songs from Under the River — **Anis Mojgani**

Spiking the Sucker Punch — **Robbie Q. Telfer**

Strange Light — **Derrick C. Brown**

Stunt Water — Buddy Wakefield

These Are the Breaks — **Idris Goodwin**

Time Bomb Snooze Alarm — **Bucky Sinister**

The Undisputed Greatest Writer of All Time — **Beau Sia**

What Learning Leaves — **Taylor Mali**

What the Night Demands — **Miles Walser**

Working Class Represent — **Cristin O'Keefe Aptowicz**

Write About an Empty Birdcage — **Elaina Ellis**

Yarmulkes & Fitted Caps — **Aaron Levy Samuels**

The Year of No Mistakes — **Cristin O'Keefe Aptowicz**

Yesterday Won't Goodbye — **Brian S. Ellis**

CPSIA information can be obtained
at www.ICGtesting.com
Printed in the USA
FSOW01n1001150916
24995FS